UNUTTERABLE VISIONS,
PERISHABLE BREATH

Otamere Guobadia is a multidisciplinary writer and poet based in London.

ISBN: 978-1-915760-49-4 (Paperback) / 978-1-915079-68-8 (Hardback)

Cover illustration: 'Burning Kiss' by Mel Odom

Edited by Andre Bagoo

Typeset by Aaron Kent

Broken Sleep Books Ltd
Rhydwen
Talgarreg
Ceredigion
SA44 4HB

Broken Sleep Books Ltd
Fair View
St Georges Road
Cornwall
PL26 7YH

Unutterable Visions, Perishable Breath

Otamere Guobadia

Broken Sleep Books

To the women in my family,

I am not often the best version of myself,
but on the days that I am it is because of you.

CONTENTS

How I did waste and exhaust my heart.

— Anne Carson, *Plainwater: Essays and Poetry*

INTRODUCTION TO A BODY TOO LONG CURATED

This is my Lusk letter; find attached the pieces of myself as they have appeared to me. Some thin and fragile as daydreams, and others with the unshakeable clarity of Gabriel's visitation.

I am a silly, changeable creature too long masquerading in balance, and this is my epistle to the unbridled. The curated body is crumbling under the weight of expectation. The mind alters, bends, shatters: these are the fountains and fragments of what remains. Our bodies are not sites of coherence: there is only madness here, and I want to close the ever-widening gap between my heart and my mouth, to write with that urgency and that fury and that wonder.

These words are perishable, dependent on the very air around them—the air that I breathe now, to never breathe again. My relationship to these truths is constantly in flux. They bear witness to my today, and not to my tomorrow, to some far-off future, and then perhaps never again a day after that.

These words are my salves. Bandages on damnation.

I have feared most the truths that revealed me to be animal. Love. Nakedness. Sex, rage, and riot. My neuroses and my insanities. My compulsions. That which seems to propel not by decision, but by the blueprint of the universe, dictated by the precise gaps between far-off stars that, even at their great distance, heat our blood.

Our bodies are ruled by the things we cannot see. Things we cannot confine, nor contain in neat, unblemished lines. Stillness is an illusion, produced by our relative micro-cosmology. We are silhouetted by a greater chaos, and this affords us our little enclave—hold water in a glass, hold breath in our bodies. In truth, we are always hurtling at great speed. By time and space, we hurtle, and we are stripped to bones and air and stars—and yet we love, and we leave a record of this love in bones and air and stars.

Tell me, darling universe, who has had the last laugh?

ICHOR

(I) TEMPO

Like gods,
As gods,
Gods,
We were,
Happy, for a time,
Runs fast,
Runs still,
Runs out.
The price of pomegranate split,
Then savoured,
A harvest, twice stolen,
Can never be returned.

Spoil and soldier of unwinnable war,
The undodgeable draft,
Willing or unwilling,
We shall be led to drink.

(II) AMORE

In an old palace,
The form and colour of midnight,
There is an oath,
Once taken in blood,
Before battle—
'If you fall, so must I. So rise.'
A rite sealed by a shared breath.
In this way,
The first kisses took place here.

Discretion is the greater part of valour,
A shame then,
I have never been the greater part of anything.
I cry in a bathtub, forsaken.
Ophelia was dead,
Long before she hit the water,
Her prince had sealed her fate.

I felt it once,
And I shall feel it again.
A humming aliveness of sound,
Mind and body,
A vast summer.
Before it was out like a flash,
Out of flesh and sight and remembering,
Irrecoverable to me,
All is night.

I cry on a plane, grateful.
Altitude is the mother of tears,
And hope.
I felt it once,

And I shall feel it again.
That honeyed blue seeping in at the edges,
Always waiting in the background of things,
To reveal itself with sleight of hand,
Out of flesh and sight and remembering.

It would seem,
Whom the gods mean to kill,
They first make love.

(III) STELLE

In death,
I will my body and its contents,
To the alchemists.
Let them search, dissect, and therein
Create love potions,
Isolate whatever defect of my blood,
The animus within it,
Leech whatever perfume,
Curse upon my house,
Find the star,
That danced above the hospital that night.
For I believe,
There is a ring of Jupiter,
Embedded in my heart,
Which like an axe,
Warps the flesh.
Take that which causes me to yearn,
Above all things,
To pine and salivate,
Howl at the moon,
That causes this want to be spent
Like a cigarette,
Like fuel,
Like water in the desert—

All I may tell you for certain:
Lovesick is a kind of sick,
And what does not make you stronger...
Kill love before it kills you.

FOR MY SISTER

I keep a photograph of you and I,
When we were young,
On my bedside table.
It is a kind of contagion magic,
A ritual,
By which I hope to overwhelm the worst parts of me
With your goodness,
Unwed the shame from my very bones.

AN INEXHAUSTIVE LIST OF LOVERS

(to be appended ad infinitum)

A comically repressed, archetypally English boy at a house party the other night, who I'm half convinced is an actual spy. An absolute sweetheart of a porn star, who told me about his plans to become a consultant, then kissed me on the hand when I said goodnight. An actor I had seen in a Fringe play weeks earlier—googled him the night before a party and found myself introduced to him while dancing. A nice girl with a bleach blonde buzz cut, who, while I was on my break during a particularly hard bartending shift, offered to make me dinner 'sometime' (Thank you. I love you. Come find me). An eccentric baby-faced actor at an out-of-town party, with whom I was deliriously forward—I kissed him and he let me sleep on his shoulder on the coach home. A tall, stunning girl in a club basement—with an outfit for years—whose friend I kissed to pacify him, and to keep her in the vicinity. Boy with the kind of face that drives all the boys crazy. Danced all night and now I can't stop thinking about that fucking face my god…! Charming, musical theatre piano-playing virtuoso in a Greenwich village dive bar, took my $5 tip with his teeth. Another actor, with hidden depths—The kind of boy that's desirous of everything and everyone, and desired by everything and everyone. Girl with long blue hair, a shade I can't quite describe, and a fur trim on an impeccable winter coat that matched said hair perfectly. A man who is, quite simply, far better than he knows. [REDACTED]. One boy winks, and angels orgy to harpsichord in minor. Him, skin pale and sickly as greeting card paper, yet eyes and face shining as an emperor. A man on the Hammersmith and City line with tattoos peeking through the sleeves of his suede jacket, and a face like one of the great war poets — quiet and sad and resolute and gay — one I imagine in his verses euphemistically calls the fever he feels for other men "an ague." A tree surgeon—last spotted suspended above Bethnal Green Road—with the rosiest cheeks I have ever seen. Young man whose barely whispered compliment about my earring I would have missed, had I not been so desperately waiting for him to say absolutely anything—

MAD HONEY

There begets a universe—
In these dreams,
I am trying to summon a harp with a feather,
Conduct an orchestra of pure night,
Raise the dead,
Set the world to rights.
I always fail.

We drink from tainted cup,
The visions
Our forebears forbade us to seek.
No man dare look!
Yet men dare look.
Green enough,
To found again
Lost legions of arabica,
Blue enough
To fill Yves' crypt,
And sink it down to night.

The hour is late,
All yet to play for.
These are doing words.
We recite small prayers,
Our courage shrinks smaller still,
Throw our bones upon the pyre,
invite judgement.

I do not take bad dreams
So lightly now,
All pain is real,
Comes from somewhere,
Finds purchase somewhere.

There are rites that must be observed.
We eat mad honey,
Let velvet wine,
Ribs like hunger stones.
When madness comes,
He takes those who do not go willingly.

FRAGMENT #24

You keep that love letter in your back pocket like a failed Chekhov's gun.

ILÉ-IFẸ̀

Trauma bleeds through generations;
Meaning,
I did not understand my father until I became him.
Who we are is in our blood,
And our blood must pursue us to the bitter end,
Must it not?
Now I know that kings are made by patricide,
And neither of us had the cunning to become kings.

I have seen her geles,
Spiral higher and more powerful
Than ship masts and skyscrapers and whipping posts.
Ṣo ti gbọ?
Our bodies are forgetting the strength and summer of their youth.

I know,
That our war drums still echo in these museums
When night falls and they believe they are returning home.
Ilé-Ifẹ̀ was a woman's invention.
I know, because I have watched my mother,
Carry generations of men on her back,
Without pausing for rest between the millennia.

FRAGMENT #2.01

You are Sagan's Galaxy.
I should know,
I traced the starlight in your back as you slept.

Lonely and unjoined light.

A GOOD PARTY

Is a wild, unknowable thing.
The storm and the teacup,
The bottle and its dregs,
The birthday cake,
Had and eaten too,
The carrot,
The stick,
The spoonful of honey,
Smoke without fire,
(But a fire if you're lucky)
First landfall,
Then later, adrift,
Beret on,
Dignity in tatters,
Improbable bruises,
Wonderful bruises,
The smile,
That the taxi driver knows you have,
But cannot acknowledge,
A promise made,
And it's breaking,
The best kept secret,
And Now a Major Motion Picture.
A phone is lost,
A phone is found,
No one dies.

FRAGMENT #99

Queerness is evidence of more. Evidence of the image and its likeness, to peek into the cauldron at the beginning of all things. It is evidence that we, in acting 'against' nature — might usurp it. Queerness is evidence of the divine — proof that all equations may be endlessly rewritten.

Queerness is water from the stone. Lazarus from the depths.
Something from nothing.

THOUGHTS ON A BODY TOO LONG CURATED

We are a glittering, perma-medicated set. A revolving door of beauty and decay—creatures, all love and no decorum.

Has glamour this latter day become dysfunctional, or has glamour always been a kind of dysfunction?

I am a secret, beneath a false drawer, set upon an illusion.

But really a kiss is the most exciting thing in the world.

I have always wanted to be perfect — everything else I have ever done has been peripheral, incidental.

Perfect posture rots the bone.

All perfect form was improvisation once.

The problem is degeneracy just looks so good on us.

All of our luxury, our excess, is paid for in someone else's deprivation, their lack, their blood.

There is nothing more cinematic than being deeply unhappy in very beautiful clothing.

I am ruled and ruined by a desire to please, to be found pleasing.

I love you, but we are the wreckage of long-battled ships, and at least one of us must be bound to something that floats.

My heart is in a consumption.

I am a miserable thing,
and all miserable things must die.

Be that which you are, and have no desire to be that which you are not.

FRAGMENT #22

The men in my congregation
Are the debris of decaying cities,
Stolen faces,
And the women are pillars
Of salt.
Do you see now
Why I could not sleep facing you?

DEMIURGE

At 2am,
In a crowded bar,
I lean over,
And in the old forbidden tongue,
Whisper my true name,
In his ear,
He does not flinch,
Instead presses his hand to my cheek,
Offers me a kiss like a cool drink of water,
Maybe we can be forgiven,
Believed,
Loved,

YELLOW BILE

FRAGMENT #33

I have met my apocalypse. I know, because he is beautiful in the way that all endings are. And now I watch him, as Mayans watched almanachs, as Faustus watches the clock—as Galileo watched for the movement of the sun only to realise it was the very ground upon which he stood that, nightly, betrayed its position in the heavens.

I watched him and I was moved. He was not.

A MAN LIES HERE STILL

I want new sheets,
And a new bed,
And a new self.
I have had the clothes,
And the manners,
Fought wars,
Attrition, shock, and awe.
A man lies here still,
Unmade.

HOTHOUSE

My dear,
What is here cannot be nigh,
Blessed are none.
The bombs are dropping now—
Kiss me,
Not for fear of loss,
But safe in the knowledge that the last thought that you will ever have,
Is how soft my lips are pressed to yours,
As Arcadia is lost forever.

I WANT

I have danced this dance for long enough to know,
"I want..." does not get.
And yet,
"I want, I want, I want!"—
Is there a truer prayer?

BUTTERSCOTCH BOYS

On the days when I feel ugly, there are beautiful boys stripping down by the river—skin stretched tight over hip bone, and collarbone, and rib cage—such is the generosity of the Oxford summer. Dandelion, Butterscotch boys. Even now, their cheeks full of champagne and river water and promised land…

It is one of those hot and intolerable evenings. Between conversations about coups and martial music, someone tells me that there are lost words elders would once use to shorten the long journey between Lagos and Benin City. By the bank of this river, I wish I had the words to speak away distance.

One Trinity afternoon, biting through the purple skin of a plum I realise that I will never be satisfied; that my teeth will always scrape unhappily at the core of things, bent on bodies still. And there have been so many of you. Cannonball, wonderwork boys. Boys, all chew and sweetness and no satisfaction.

love me love me love me love me love me love me love me love me love me
love me love me love me love me love me love me love me love me love me
love me love me love me love me love me love me love me love me love me
love me love me love me love me love me love me love me love me love me
love me love me love me love me love me love me love me love me love me
love me love me love me love me love me love me love me love me love me
love me love me love me love me love me love me love me love me love me
love me love me love me love me love me love me love me love me love me
love me love me love me love me love me love me love me love me love me
love me love me love me love me love me love me love me love me love me
love me love me love me love me love me love me love me love me love me
love me love me love me love me love me love me love me love me love me
love me love me love me love me love me love me love me love me love me
love me love me love me love me love me love me love me love me love me
love me love me love me love me love me love me love me love me love me
love me love me love me love me love me love me love me love me love me
love me love me love me love me love me love me love me love me love me
love me love me love me love me love me love me love me love me love me
love me love me love me love me love me love me love me love me love me
love me love me love me love me love me love me love me love me love me
love me love me love me love me love me love me love me love me love me
love me love me love me love me love me love me love me love me love me
love me love me love me love me love me love me love me love me love me
love me love me love me love me love me love me love me love me love me
love me love me love me love me love me love me love me love me love me
love me love me love me love me love me love me love me love me love me
love me love me love me love me love me love me love me love me love me
love me love me love me love me love me love me love me love me love me
love me love me love me love me love me love me love me love me love me
love me love me love me love me love me love me love me love me love me
love me love me love me love me love me love me love me love me love me
love me love me love me love me love me love me love me love me love me
love me love me love me love me love me love me love me love me love me
love me love me love me love me love me love me love me love me love me
love me love me love me love me love me love me love me love me love me
love me love me love me love me love me love me love me love me love me

MY NEW YEAR'S RESOLUTIONS

To be less beholden to beauty;
To accept it less as currency in lieu of character.
To find worship in ordinary and extraordinary people alike.
To be something more tender and less vain.
Wear more blush.

FRAGMENT #6

Desire is a false mirror. I looked upon a lake of fire and sweat, expecting divine truth to be reflected back to me, and all I saw—what I received—was a great unwell persisting beneath the surface; charred bodies, echo without source, a mad and rooted shadow calling to 'self'. I am at the mercy of the thing I love. I pray still for better days.

FETCH ME THE LIGHT

Bring me love,
And all its perfume,
Fetch me the light,
And the thing beneath the light.
If we are owed life,
Then we are owed love—
Does the latter,

Not follow from the former?

FRAGMENT #197

Mine is a body beholden to chaos. To interferent intimacies, to reels in Knightsbridge churches, to hands held, friends kissed, beds occupied and fallen into and out of—

FRAGMENT #1249

When we arrived in the city that year, it was the beginning of all time. Hitherto, God had halted the hourglass. Our bodies only erupted into existence on crossing town lines and pressing hand and foot firmly to sandstone, and ambition, and riot. No doubt we had lived in some sense before—

But here we became.

In those days, we cursed our tutors, our fathers, and our lovers, for the cardinal sin of not embodying all three—whispered imprecatory prayers into the cheap glasses of cheap wine that gave us the courage to fuck strangers—and each other. We knew nothing about nothing then, and I know nothing about nothing now, but wine gave us conviction where faith could not—and 'love' did all the rest. Those early years, every last one of us looked at the other as if through cracked, technicolour glass— kaleidoscopic visions: shining, distorted, magnified—and we called it love.

And in the becoming...

All I truly remember about those years is that I sang badly, and wanted you too much—like sundials want sun—and I drank too much, and I was so foolish, and I am so sorry for everything I have become.

FRAGMENT #54

It's a 26 degree night in Benin City and my mother is on the dance floor throwing solo shapes to disco music while the barbecue simmers away in the background and these are the things that scrape up against utopia.

FRAGMENT #361

So much of my desire often hinges entirely on circumstance, on the silly minutiae unrelated to physical attraction—lights, music, noise. More in love with petrichor than people.

And yet still so deeply, deeply in love with people.

FRAGMENT #43

I heard all fascists are bad kissers.

FRAGMENT #55

The people you love do not live forever and that is the first tragedy.

A kiss is a unit of measurement—how we count the courage it takes to close the gaps between people.

FRAGMENT #1

Sound fractures, time fractures, this unnatural world threatens to overwhelm you. You press your chest to his and his heartbeat is as a ravishing, piercing constant. A man built of green earth and sweet-smelling salts. An anchor, an antidote of a man.

A foil to your poison.

CONTRADICTIONS

I.
All speech is incantation.
Do we not,
With our every ordinary word,
Summon gods and beasts in small places,
Curdle starlight,
Kill out the things we love?

II.
All that is within us,
Is ineffable.
Words fail us,
The moment we
begin to speak them.

III.
Do not wait,
For perfect words,
They will not come.
Go into the world,
Be in the world.

BLACK BILE

ON LIMBO

And acid tongues,
Shall meet their end,
On the very swords,
That carved sharp such wit.
For Peter is at the gate,
And Paul will not be denied his due—
I see no way out.

These days are about mitigation,
About stemming the flow of blood.
There can be no happiness here,
Only the prevention of some deeper loss.
Poverty is my master,
And I have sworn,
To have no masters.

In the end,
Salvation either comes or it does not.
There is no halfway heaven.

FRAGMENT #27

Forgive your most disorderly host,
Forgive this night,
Come to more harm than good.

THE FLAME, THE FAG, OR THE ASH

I.
I think fireworks speak to our atoms,
Commune with us on the particulate,
They touch something within us that is before time itself.

II.
In a flower market,
A man takes a break from his stall.
He cradles a cigarette between fore and middle finger,
Gentler, gentler, gentler,
Than I can long recall being held.
It is hard to imagine it alight,
Against the slick grey-making air,
And yet its embers are glowing,
Like the hair of a pre-Raphaelite woman,
Or the turning leaves,
Or some other inadequate comparator
For recollecting in words,
That which may never be so moving as the sight itself.

III.
I think they called it Greek,
Before it was Reichstag,
And then later Manhattan.
I am all too familiar with improbable fires.
The kind that burn even in water,
The kind that refuse to be drowned.
Am I the flame, the fag, or the ash?

FRAGMENT #72

This is my jeremiad. What can follow this but ruin?

FRAGMENT #23

You're all terrible, and I love you.

FRAGMENT #30

You think you can party to avoid the reckoning but maybe the party is the reckoning.

FRAGMENT #222

I hate the slack in old turtlenecks,
The great distance between our fingers,
Things have never quite clung to me as they should.
It is easy enough,
To have a spark,
Hard to make love stick.
Who knows what would have taken in the end.

A POULTICE FOR TRUE NATURE

Inhale steel, malice, bitter lemon,
Exhale citrus, righteousness, sainthood.
Tree meet axe,
Principality meet power.
Shoot the bloody messenger.

FRAGMENT #136

All the people I love,
Now work too hard and leave parties early.

FRAGMENT #14

Is there not world enough for us,
Or is there too much world?
The heart beats,
Wants to beat,
But the rib cage,
Constrains the heart,
The flesh constrains the ribcage,
The constitution falters,
Air cannot hope to rout such blight,
Foul dust pumps into extremities,
Pray now only for miracles of amber.

Even the most unliving fossil,
Once strode the world,
In search of touch and succour,
Entreated some connection.
There is an appeasement,
A balm,
Something that is called to fill it,
For every aching gap.
Believe you me.

Life calls itself into existence,
Out of a mirror universe of nothings.
We wrote the bible, the God, and the man.
Built the garden,
Then banished ourselves from it.
What might we still do now,
That midnight calls at our door?

THE SEVENTH DAY

(Desire's First Victim)

And on the seventh day,
God did not rest—
Though all accounts have at this time,
Grown apocryphal.
Instead,
I believe,
He carved your name into the valleys and the hillsides and the mountain-tops,
Tattooed it on his left thigh,
And then forbade tattooing,
Stood with a boombox above his head,
Outside a window in Elysium,
Painted your waif face on ocean beds,
Wrote sonnets,
Begged for your love,
Cried returning home from Eden,
Multiplied his multitudes,
And still felt empty for want of you.
Invented Sin,
Felt lonely in his own perfection,
Drowned the world in his tears,
Devised the apple,
Fed the five thousand,
And then five thousand more,
Drank till he forgot,
Appointed the angels,
Threw himself in a well,
And was lost for all time.

PHLEGM

(IV) GANG OF SODOMITICAL WRETCHES

(From This Great Height)

Like songbirds,
Drowned in Armagnac,
There are some embraces,
Too sweet for even heaven to see.
And yet—on this night,
We hide not even from God himself.

What if this is something we invented?
Oh, how powerful we would be then!
To think men into God,
Long the Devil into the world,
Bind the bright stars and the clear water.

From this great height,
And at dazzling speed,
Are we not the land?
And the story of the land?
Piety is the first denial,
And what we seek here,
Is the means to an aesthetic rapture.

Never met an advertisement,
That couldn't make me want something;
Never met an altar I couldn't fall down,
And worship.

NOBLESSE OBLIGE

(The Very Heart of the Matter)

By my good fortune,
This day,
And your unluck,
I have found myself,
In your heart—
Cupbearer,
Knight and keeper of its realm,
Unworthy.
A knife,
A bomb,
A spy in red vestments.
And so I devote myself
To betterment,
A flourishing
Of garden and gardener.
Let neither of us,
Your godshone countenance, waste.

FRAGMENT #95

Things are found, varnished, worshipped.
Things are lost, discarded, abandoned.
The way of all things.

You will be known again.

FRAGMENT #1001

The kiss is the enemy of the partition.
Partition may prevent kiss,
But kiss dissolves all need for partition.

If we,
This strange class,
Are too survive this attrition,
There can be no enmity between us.

FRAGMENT #77

'I love you' is what we say when there is nothing left to say.
Or perhaps because there is everything left to say and no time ever enough to say it. 'I love you'—it is an approximation. An invocation. To condense all life into a single breath.

SHORTCOMINGS

You think you know your own heart,
Then the metaphor fails,
And you are left,
With the corpse,
Of the thing you were trying to say.
I have the sharper knife,
The slighter flesh.
There can be no cure
For that which ails me—
My own heart poisons the well.

FRAGMENT #89

Maybe We Were Just Bad People: A Memoir

FRAGMENT #0

How different things would be if we could go back and arrest that first mistake—prevent the visitation of our first cruelty, from which all other cruelties followed.

NO MORE

No more many and splendid gifts of silver and self,
No more 54th street psychics,
No priests,
Nor prophets,
Nor portents,
No bones,
No omens,
No waters,
Nor the things felt in them.
Give us over
Only to those who might possess secret knowledge,
Of how we might live in these present times.
Happiness must flow from this moment,
And banish the touch-hungry tomorrows.
All history was once a future king,
Fight for the now.

THIS FAIR CITY

Londinium,
Not-the-year of our Lord,
For any gods have long since,
Abandoned our little settlement
To ruin—
If they ever came here at all.

City of obelisks,
Columns and cenotaphs,
Stolen, fragmented
As mine own heart.

But here, I may touch
Roman Roads and Roman Walls,
Be made whole by the past—
By others and another's past.
This is my only restitution,
I cannot be made whole
By my own.

LOVE IS A THING YOU EAT, LOVE IS A THING THAT EATS YOU.

I am still trying to fortify my flesh—scrubbing the lust off of my skin; trying to hold together a body insistent upon discarding the unforgivable parts of itself. I am remembering the taste of strawberry punch, the nonsensical words and circumlocution that accompanied the slightly irritating scent of Drakkar Noir, and fragments of Imperial Leather between meals too big to finish; peanut butter on Graham crackers; warm nutmeg gaining purpose in my mother's hands. This is not just metaphor—Love transfigures food into something greater. Loneliness is not profound anymore; no nuance in shades of blue and grey, no message in bargain-bin cardboard supermarket sandwiches. It is a dangerous and unknowable thing to be a person in search of redemption. I must risk a backwards glance. I do not try and make sense of these things anymore. These are my islands of innocence.

Under these orange spires, cheap champagne— false firmament—disappears my time, time fashioning lovers into friends, friends into strangers; trail of firewater burning bridges from tongue to nostril, chasing sweat out onto these nevermean streets, their stone resembling candied glass under this very *real* firmament. Sampling too many lips: flavours too ephemeral to survive long and unfed between these seasons, not enough bloom to be reborn when we smell this cold stone after a long absence. Never enough to overpower my own pretentious, whisky-orange breath. Your still lingering scent: all synthesis and no nature; patriarch's poison coursing over our skin repellent and infused with shame. Journeys through food: recurrence of the inauthentic orient, the overpowering coriander medicated to us on history-soaked wooden benches; light pouring through stained glass windows like boiled sweet aperitif.

There have been lovers in every flavour. His clumsiness manifest in his tongue, yours in your eyes—the smell of vodka the morning after scenting pilgrimage; the blue bitterness of sunrise, and fermented jalapeños wafting regret. Peppermint oil and citrus, and the Egyptians' old cure returning the sun to your voice; still a pale imitation of all Her fire. Think on the boldness of her flesh, the shrill in her green dress, the kink of her hair, the curt in her voice, the sting of her sass like lime on our bruised lips! Empires of red wine — staining lips, dyeing tongues, reviving stony spirits with our own rich laughter, bringing you back from the depths, sinking you lower than you ever imagined, the way that only grape and witchcraft could.

Warm cider— unmitigated, bountiful love, indestructible trust, such unending brightness, a queen abdicating all propriety for love, absolving all responsibility, inviting utter chaos. Earthy, bitter, Jäger—driving him to flight, and us to fight, and to simmer and to fight, and to smile and to fight, and to kiss and to fight and to fight...
More chemistry with purpose, mixology inviting too much coolness and too little disquiet, flavours not bold enough to incite riot. Cosmopolitan cool. Martini-bitter breath—

This is turning into one of those letters. I am desperately trying to be something that you can be proud of.

I am sorry that I am so empty. I love you.
You know that, don't you?

In hospital rooms, strange white smoke opening my airways.

Worlds away, her voodoo punch, heritage of her caramel skin—her witches' brew, extra strong by the full moon. Black coffee on the wrong side of sunlight fueling your crises; the warmth of tea; medicinal, varied, omnipresent, bitter, sweet, fragrant; at once cure, and regret and burrowing nest, bosom, and friend's embrace. Tears slick and scent my path like petrichor. Mouths thick with theory, and sloth, and rage, and undoing words. It is romance, unrejoicing but true to form. Boys with scars like bruised fruit. Newfound rebellion. And I remember it all. The taste of your collarbone, the muscovado sugar of her eyes, the flour on their brows as they laugh bloody murder. In exile, the saccharine of their port comporting without propriety. I delight in the foreignness of my body; the rolling strangeness of your skin, your cinnamon grin...

This is my revisionist history. The paint may never be so bright as it is in the photograph; your fondness of me never so compelling; past and future not so symmetrical. Mountains of sugar and rivers of wine and molasses rain all turned to decay. My empires are no longer burning.

AN ADDENDUM

Joy bleeds through generations,
Like an X on a map,
Like buried treasure,
Like city living,
Like Hercules,
And San Fernando Valley,
And graham crackers,
And peanut butter,
Like the busiest of towns,
And dial-up modems,
And gold stars,
Like a fort,
made from a green suitcase,
Like Brass Lamp,
And Blue Tack,
And Sundays at the boat club,
Like Road 40, House 42,
Like his blazer over my shoulders,
Like the hem of her lace a healing thing,
Like headties eclipsing the broad sun,
Like a god of war,
More sun than flaming arrow,
Come to love not conquer,
Yet with kind brow,
And warlike wits,
She floats astride us.
Like a kid's red Jeep Wrangler,
Like walkie talkies,
And strawberry punch,
And fading and trodden constellations,
Like Camelot,
And agbadas,
And agbalumo seeds,

And coral beads around our necks,
One beautiful thing after another.
To love is to remember,
To seek out,
To make new.
The best is come,
Is said and done,
The best is yet to be.

ACKNOWLEDGEMENTS

Thank you to Mr Bevan, who cleft open my mind and poured words and light into its darkest corners—a man who was kind to me at a time when I found it impossible to be kind to myself. I remember every word and every phrase you spoke, every bit of genius you imparted in those days, and how little you asked of us in return. I would not be half the writer I am, nor have even a modicum of my success without your divine intervention.

To Winnie, my rock, my anchor. To Sovereign House, and all who passed through its doors, and to our days and nights of legend. To my friends and family, who have helped keep the lights on literally and figuratively, who have believed and continued to believe in me—you have sustained me more than you could ever know, in more ways than I could ever pay you back for.

To Zoe Ross, my literary agent, who plucked me from obscurity (where I arguably remain and am content to) and stuck by me through years of gestation and false starts. Thank you for your patience and for pushing me to leave this mark on the world. Olivia you have been an absolute dream, and I thank you for tolerating my madness and sadness with aplomb.

To my lovers—those who have broken my heart and bruised my ego, and those whose hearts and egos I have bruised and broken—I forgive you; I hope you forgive me. Thank you for the many wonderful kisses.

Yours eternally,
Otamere

LAY OUT YOUR UNREST

Milton Keynes UK
Ingram Content Group UK Ltd.
UKHW041158181223
434583UK00001B/1

9 781915 079688